EDGE
BOOKS

STARS OF PRO WRESTLING

BATISTA

BY TIM O'SHEI

Consultant:
Mike Johnson, Writer
PWInsider.com

Capstone
press

Mankato, Minnesota

Edge Books are published by Capstone Press,
151 Good Counsel Drive, P.O. Box 669, Mankato, Minnesota 56002.
www.capstonepress.com
Copyright © 2010 by Capstone Press, a Capstone Publishers company.

Books published by Capstone Press are manufactured with paper
containing at least 10 percent post-consumer waste.

Library of Congress Cataloging-in-Publication Data
O'Shei, Tim.
　Batista / By Tim O'Shei.
　p. cm. — (Edge books. Stars of pro wrestling)
　Includes bibliographical references and index.
　Summary: "Describes the life and career of pro wrestler Dave Batista" —
Provided by publisher.
　ISBN 978-1-4296-3349-9 (library binding)
　1. Batista, Dave, 1969– — Juvenile literature. 2. Wrestlers — United States
— Biography — Juvenile literature. I. Title.
GV119.B37O75 2010
796.812092 — dc22
[B]   2008055908

Editorial Credits
Angie Kaelberer, editor; Ted Williams, designer; Jo Miller, media researcher

Photo Credits
Alamy/Allstar Picture Library, 7, 25
Getty Images Inc./AFP/Paul J. Richards, 9; Gaye Gerard, 29; Russell Turiak,
　11; WireImage/Djamilla Rosa Cochran, 22; WireImage/Don Arnold, 15;
　WireImage/J. Shearer, 6; WireImage/Leon Halip, 19
Globe Photos/John Barrett, 21, 27; Milan Ryba, cover, 5
Landov LLC/Orlando Sentinel/MCT/Red Huber, 18
Newscom, 13; WENN/Carrie Devorah, 26
Shutterstock/Lori Martin, 16

Design Elements
Shutterstock/amlet; Henning Janos; J. Danny; kzww

TABLE OF CONTENTS

Chapter 1

WRESTLING FOR THE CHAMPIONSHIP

On April 3, 2005, the Staples Center in Los Angeles, California, was jammed. It was time for the final event of the night. The crowd was riled up, and the action was about to explode.

This was WrestleMania, the biggest World Wrestling Entertainment (WWE) event. The last match would settle a **feud** that had been brewing for months. The WWE World Heavyweight Champion, Triple H, would defend his belt against Batista.

The two men were friends. They once were part of a group called Evolution. They had traveled together with fellow Evolution member, Ric Flair. Triple H and Flair were wrestling legends. Batista was newer to the sport. He learned all he could from Triple H and Flair. Now Batista was about to unleash his knowledge and skills on Triple H.

feud — a long-running quarrel

Batista was pumped to wrestle Triple H for the World Heavyweight title.

Triple H entered the ring. Backstage, Batista heard the music and the roar of the crowd. As he made his way to the ring, a tear welled in his eye. He had started in the wrestling business only five years ago. Now he needed to prove that he could win the World Heavyweight Championship.

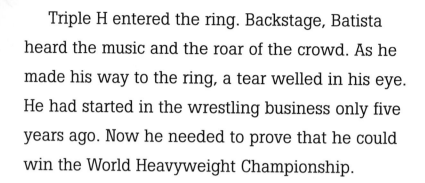

WRESTLING FACT

Batista's last name is really spelled "Bautista." He drops the "u" for wrestling because he thinks Batista sounds tougher.

At WrestleMania, Batista backed Triple H into the corner of the ring.

Batista showed his strength by tossing Triple H to the mat.

Chapter 2

GROWING UP TOUGH

Batista grew up in one of the toughest sections of Washington, D.C. The Capitol building, where Congress works, was a short drive away. The White House was just up the street. But Batista's neighborhood wasn't rich or elegant. It was actually quite dangerous.

EARLY LIFE

Batista was born January 18, 1969. He was named David Michael after his father, but people call him Dave for short. Dave has a younger sister, Donna. Dave's parents separated when he was a small child. He and his sister lived with their mother, who is also named Donna. Dave knew his father, but they didn't have a strong relationship. Dave thought his dad wasn't interested in him.

Dave grew up in the large city of Washington, D.C.

Dave's mom worked nights. From a young age, the kids were on their own while she was at work. Dave and his sister weren't allowed to leave their yard. People were robbed, injured, or killed in their area of the city every day.

When Dave was 7, Donna moved the family to San Francisco, California. A year later, Dave's father convinced Donna to move the family back to Washington. Soon after they returned, a person was murdered in their front yard. Not long after, two more people were killed in their neighborhood. It was more violence than Donna could handle. She moved the family back to San Francisco.

WRESTLING FAN

Dave loved to watch pro wrestling on TV. His favorite wrestler was The Warlord from World Championship Wrestling (WCW). Many fans cheered for **babyface** wrestlers. But Dave preferred The Warlord and other **heels** like Mr. Fuji and "Ravishing" Rick Rude.

babyface — a wrestler who acts as a hero in the ring
heel — a wrestler who acts as a villain in the ring

Former wrestler "Ravishing" Rick Rude was one of young Dave's favorites.

In his own life, Dave was a bit of a heel himself. He didn't like going to school and often skipped it. He got in trouble for fighting and stealing. He was arrested and spent brief periods in juvenile detention. Dave's mother was upset by his behavior. When he was 13, she sent him to live with his father in Arlington, Virginia. But Dave kept skipping school and getting into trouble.

High School Dropout

Dave's behavior didn't improve when he was in high school. He was sent to a group home, which helped a little. He also joined the wrestling team for a year, which he enjoyed. But in his senior year, his poor grades kept him off the team. He never graduated from high school.

Dave's young adult life didn't start well either. He got in trouble for fighting and using illegal drugs. Dave even spent some time in jail. The only positive thing in his life was that he started weight training. Always tall and skinny, Dave packed on about 50 pounds (23 kilograms) of muscle. The gym became one of his favorite places. The skills he learned there would one day help make him a superstar. But he had many challenges to face first.

WRESTLING FACT

Batista suffers from asthma, a medical condition that causes him to sometimes have problems breathing. His asthma makes his wrestling career even more difficult.

Dave has used weight training to build muscles since he was a teenager.

Chapter 3

FROM HARD TIMES TO STARDOM

When Dave was 20, he married a woman named Glenda. Their first daughter, Keilani, was born in 1990. Two years later, they had a second daughter, Athena. But the marriage wasn't happy. Dave and Glenda divorced soon after Athena's birth. Dave was determined to be a better father than his father had been. He stayed in contact with his daughters and even had custody of them at one time.

Dave worked a variety of jobs in his 20s. He was a lifeguard. He was a security worker in bars. He even worked as a bodyguard for a few famous people.

While working out at a gym, Dave met pro wrestlers Curt Hennig and Joseph Laurinaitis. They told Dave that his large size and muscular build would be good for a career in wrestling. He took their advice and started training even harder.

Dave thought his size and build might be good for a career in wrestling.

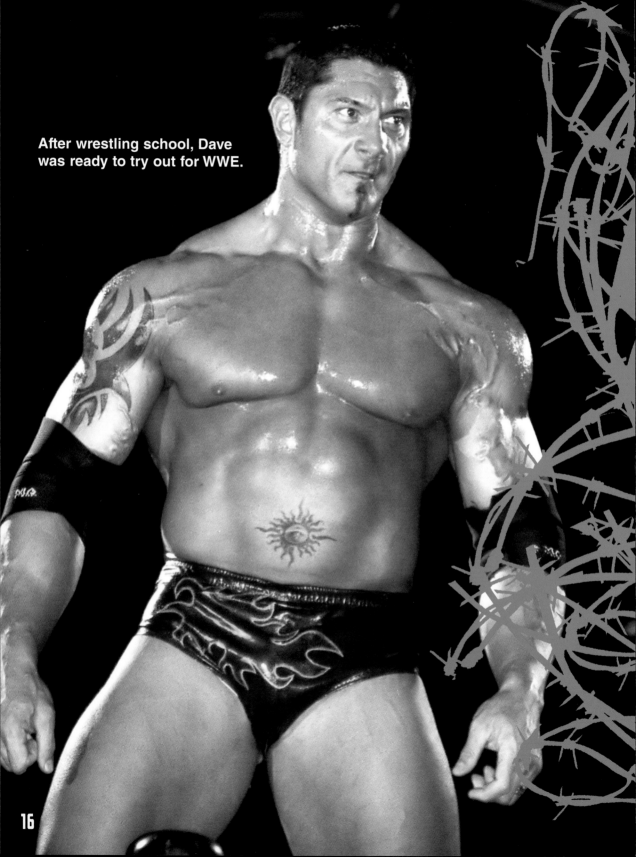

After wrestling school, Dave was ready to try out for WWE.

Dave tried out for World Championship Wrestling (WCW). This company was based in Atlanta, Georgia. The trainer told Dave that he wasn't good enough to be a wrestler and kicked him out of the gym. But Dave wasn't discouraged. Instead, he became even more determined to become a wrestler.

STAR STUDENT

In 1998, Dave moved to Allentown, Pennsylvania. Dave enrolled in the Wild Samoan Training Center. A former professional wrestler named Afa Anoa'i ran this wrestling school. Anoa'i liked Dave's size, his look, and his determination. He gave Dave many one-on-one lessons.

Paying for the school and expenses was not cheap. It cost around $150,000. Dave couldn't afford it, but two of his friends loaned him the money. After several months, Anoa'i thought Dave was ready to turn pro. He arranged for Dave to try out with WWE.

WRESTLING FACT

Batista was 30 when he started wrestling. Most wrestlers begin their careers in their late teens or early 20s.

A RIVER MONSTER

Dave's second tryout went much better than his first. WWE signed Dave to a developmental contract. He joined a small company called Ohio Valley Wrestling (OVW). Wrestlers Randy Orton and John Cena also got their start there. Dave wrestled as Leviathan, a monster from the Ohio River.

Wrestlers in OVW make little money. But Dave learned a lot. He had to make Leviathan seem real. Dave growled and made scary faces. And he had the strength to easily defeat most of his opponents.

WWE wrestler Randy Orton also got his start in OVW.

Making it Big

Most wrestlers don't begin their careers in WWE. They have to start small. Many, including Batista, attend a wrestling school where they learn basic moves, how to fall, and how to create an interesting character. From there, wrestlers move on to a small league. Batista wrestled in Ohio Valley Wrestling, which is based in Kentucky.

WWE invites the best wrestlers from the smaller companies to try out. If WWE officials like what they see, they offer the wrestler a developmental contract. That means WWE will track the wrestler's progress. The wrestler may be called up to wrestle in a WWE match or two. The best developmental wrestlers, like Batista, get a chance to work full time in WWE.

ON TO WWE

Dave's two years of hard work in OVW paid off. In 2002, WWE asked him to appear on their TV shows. His first job was to act as a bodyguard to Reverend D-Von, a preacher. Deacon Batista, as he was called, carried a cashbox attached to a chain strapped around his neck. As part of his character, he collected money for Reverend D-Von's church. Other than a few minor scuffles, Deacon Batista didn't wrestle. He just looked threatening.

Even though Dave didn't get to wrestle much, D-Von taught him a lot about the wrestling business. But after a few months, Dave's in-ring relationship with D-Von ended. Dave wasn't sure what his future in WWE would be.

When he joined WWE, Batista teamed with D-Von Dudley (right), who wrestled as Reverend D-Von.

Randy Orton (left), Batista, and Ric Flair (right) were part of Evolution.

WRESTLING MOVE

Batista bomb — the wrestler puts the opponent's head between his thighs, flips the opponent up onto his shoulders, and then drops to the mat with a bodyslam

EVOLUTION

In 2003, Dave became part of a four-man **stable** of heels called Evolution. His partners were Rick Flair, Triple H, and Randy Orton. Now known as simply "Batista," he wowed crowds with his *Batista bomb*. He became a star, winning the World Tag Team Championship in December 2003 with Ric Flair.

For a year and a half, Evolution made wrestling fans everywhere boo. But then something changed. In November 2004, Batista and Triple H got into a big argument on live TV. Within weeks, Batista left Evolution. His feud continued with Triple H. More and more, fans were cheering Batista. He was quickly becoming a babyface. And he was headed toward a showdown with Triple H.

stable — a group of wrestlers who wrestle together and protect each other

Chapter 4

BATISTA THE CHAMPION

The big moment with Triple H came during WrestleMania in 2005. Following his entrance, Triple H took command in the ring. He overpowered Batista for most of the match, partly because of help from Ric Flair. When Batista staggered, Triple H prepared him for the *Pedigree*. But Batista wrestled out of it, surprising Triple H with a slam.

Batista took control, leading Triple H up to the Batista bomb. As he lifted Triple H into the air, a thought went through Batista's mind, "I can't believe this is happening." He slammed Triple H to the mat. The referee pounded his palm on the mat three times. Batista was the WWE World Heavyweight Champion.

Batista defeated Triple H to win the World Heavyweight title at WrestleMania.

WRESTLING MOVE

Pedigree — a wrestler holds the opponent face down and drops to his knees, slamming the opponent's head to the mat

A Quick Rise

Shortly after WrestleMania, WWE shuffled the assignments of several wrestlers. Batista moved from *Raw* to *SmackDown!* He started feuds with John Bradshaw Layfield (JBL) and then with Eddie Guerrero. But he managed to hang on to his title.

In a January 2006 match against Mark Henry, Batista tore his triceps. An injured champ can't keep the title, so Batista had to give up the belt. He had an operation on his arm and took six months off to recover. But he returned in time to win back the title from King Booker in November 2006.

Batista feuded with JBL (left) in 2005.

A Filipino Celebrity

On his left shoulder, Batista has a tattoo of the flag of the Republic of the Philippines. His father's family comes from the Philippines. That connection has made Batista a big celebrity there. Thousands of fans greeted him when he visited the Philippines in September 2006. People even held a parade for him in the capital city of Manila. Batista said he has never had such an exciting welcome anywhere else in the world.

CHASING THE CHAMPIONSHIPS

Batista held on to his title until WrestleMania in April 2007, when he lost it to Undertaker. The belt changed hands twice in the next three months. Batista won it back from The Great Khali in September 2007. In December, he lost it to Edge. On October 26, 2008, Batista defeated Chris Jericho for the title. He held it only one week before Jericho won it back.

In professional wrestling, championships come and go. The real sign of a wrestler's success is how long he or she stays in the sport. Batista has been injured several times. He's undergone painful surgeries and rehabilitation. But so far, he has always made it back to the ring.

Some wrestlers, like Ric Flair, are able to compete for 20 or 30 years. Because Batista started at an older age, he may never achieve that goal. But his name will be alongside stars like Flair and Undertaker in wrestling history. Like them, Batista is a legend.

Batista has managed to overcome
injuries and return to the ring.

GLOSSARY ★ ★ ★ ★ ★ ★

babyface (BAY-bee-fayss) — a wrestler who acts as a hero in the ring

developmental contract (duh-VEHL-up-ment-tuhl KAHN-tract) — a deal in which a wrestler is paid to compete in a smaller league as a way to train for a bigger league like WWE

feud (FYOOD) — a long-running quarrel between two people or groups of people

heel (HEEL) — a wrestler who acts as a villain in the ring

rehabilitation (ree-huh-bil-uh-TAY-shun) — therapy that helps people recover their health or abilities

stable (STAY-buhl) — a group of wrestlers who protect each other during matches and sometimes wrestle together

tricep (TRY-sep) — the muscle along the back of the upper arm

READ MORE

Kaelberer, Angie Peterson. *The Nature Boy: Pro Wrestler Ric Flair.* Pro Wrestlers. Mankato, Minn.: Capstone Press, 2004.

Kaelberer, Angie Peterson. *Triple H: Pro Wrestler Hunter Hearst Helmsley.* Pro Wrestlers. Mankato, Minn.: Capstone Press, 2003.

Shields, Brian, and Kevin Sullivan. *WWE Encyclopedia.* New York: DK Publishing, 2009.

INTERNET SITES

FactHound offers a safe, fun way to find Internet sites related to this book. All of the sites on FactHound have been researched by our staff.

Here's all you do:

Visit *www.facthound.com*

FactHound will fetch the best sites for you!

INDEX ★ ★ ★ ★ ★ ★ ★